A BOOK OF INFOGRAPHICS

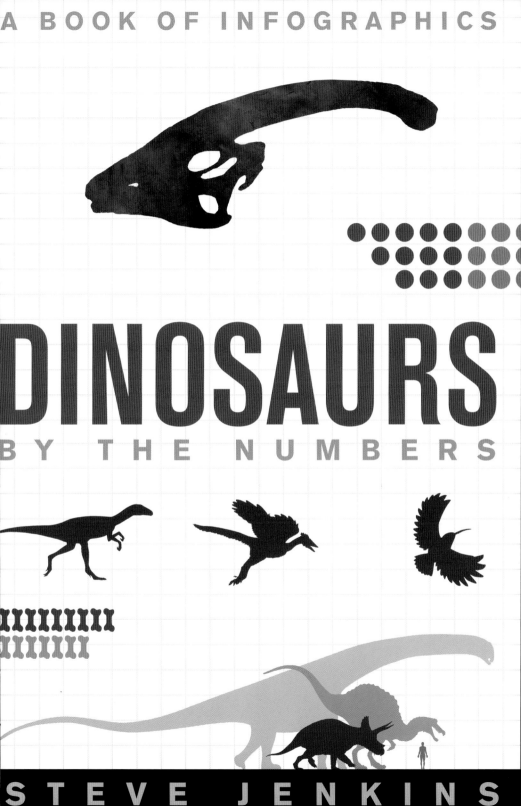

DINOSAURS
BY THE NUMBERS

STEVE JENKINS

Contents

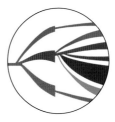

About dinosaur names
Most dinosaurs have scientific names that are not easy to pronounce. There is more information about these dinosaurs and a guide to pronouncing their names on page 36.

Dinosaurs ruled the earth for more than 150 million years. Some were small, speedy, and covered with feathers. Others were huge, armor-plated beasts. There were fierce predators with terrifying teeth and claws. A gigantic plant-eating dinosaur was the largest animal to ever live on land. These amazing animals lived all over the world. Then, about 66 million years ago, almost all of them vanished.

This book uses infographics—illustrations, charts, and graphs—to show what dinosaurs looked like, how they lived, and what happened to them. And it introduces the dinosaurs that are still alive today.

* Words in blue can be found in the glossary on page 38.

Meet the dinosaurs

Some dinosaurs ate plants . . .

Lambeosaurus

Dinosaurs were a kind of reptile.

Like all reptiles, they laid eggs.

Some dinosaurs had feathers.

Unlike other reptiles, many dinosaurs were warm-blooded.

. . . and some ate other dinosaurs.

Allosaurus

The first reptiles lived about 310 million years ago.

Dinosaurs appeared 235 million years ago.

Most dinosaurs went extinct 66 million years ago . . .

. . . but one kind of dinosaur survived.

Living dinosaurs

Scientists tell us that birds are actually a group of dinosaurs. They survived the mass extinction that happened 66 million years ago.

Caudipteryx was a feathered dinosaur that lived 125 million years ago. Its skeleton looks a lot like that of a modern bird.

Caudipteryx, a pigeon, and a human hand

Birds are living dinosaurs!

Birds evolved from predatory dinosaurs that could walk upright, such as **Coelophysis**. It lived 200 million years ago.

Archeopteryx, a feathered dinosaur, was one of the first birds. It lived 150 million years ago.

Today there are some 10,000 species of birds—living dinosaurs.

When did the dinosaurs live?

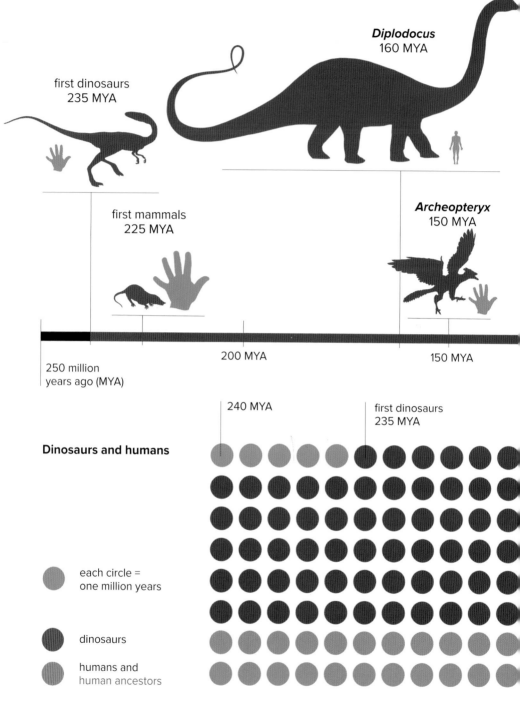

Diplodocus
160 MYA

first dinosaurs
235 MYA

first mammals
225 MYA

Archeopteryx
150 MYA

250 million
years ago (MYA)

200 MYA

150 MYA

240 MYA

first dinosaurs
235 MYA

Dinosaurs and humans

each circle =
one million years

dinosaurs

humans and
human ancestors

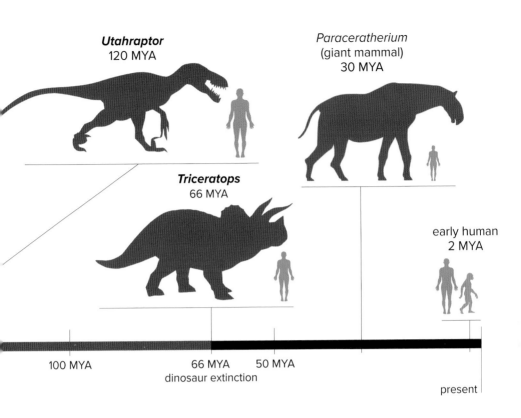

Utahraptor
120 MYA

Paraceratherium
(giant mammal)
30 MYA

Triceratops
66 MYA

early human
2 MYA

100 MYA

66 MYA
dinosaur extinction

50 MYA

present

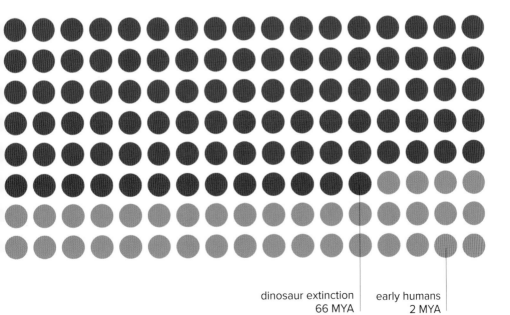

dinosaur extinction
66 MYA

early humans
2 MYA

How big were the dinosaurs?

Dinosaurs, a few modern-day animals, and an adult human are shown at the same scale.

Parasaurolophus

great white shark

Ankylosaurus

Triceratops

grizzly bear

Tyrannosaurus rex

Therizinosaurus

blue whale

dinosaurs

modern-day animals

Stegosaurus

giraffe

Dilophosaurus

Gallimimus

Maiasaura

Archeopteryx

Spinosaurus

African elephant

saltwater crocodile

Velociraptor

Patagotitan

adult human

How fast were the dinosaurs?

Estimated speed in miles per hour
(mph) and kilometers per hour (kph)

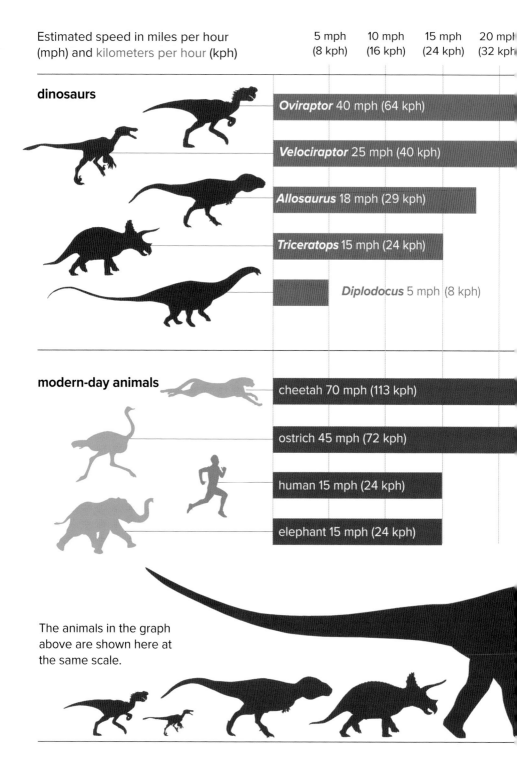

	5 mph (8 kph)	10 mph (16 kph)	15 mph (24 kph)	20 mph (32 kph)

dinosaurs

Oviraptor 40 mph (64 kph)

Velociraptor 25 mph (40 kph)

Allosaurus 18 mph (29 kph)

Triceratops 15 mph (24 kph)

Diplodocus 5 mph (8 kph)

modern-day animals

cheetah 70 mph (113 kph)

ostrich 45 mph (72 kph)

human 15 mph (24 kph)

elephant 15 mph (24 kph)

The animals in the graph
above are shown here at
the same scale.

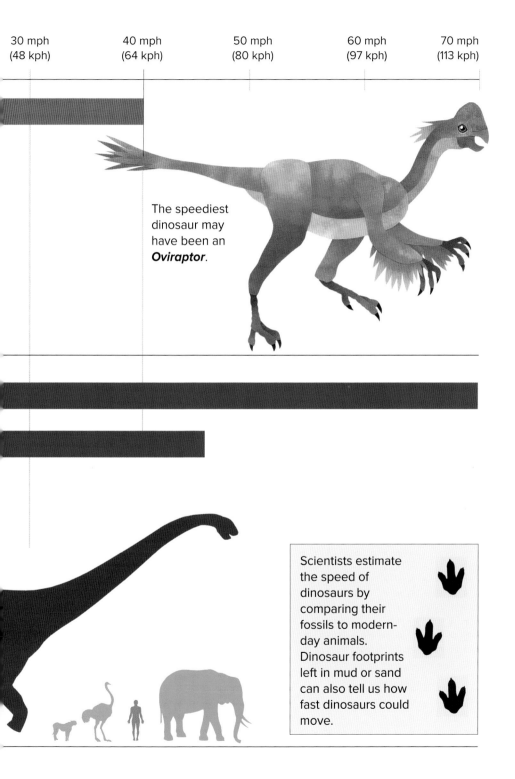

| 30 mph
(48 kph) | 40 mph
(64 kph) | 50 mph
(80 kph) | 60 mph
(97 kph) | 70 mph
(113 kph) |

The speediest dinosaur may have been an **Oviraptor**.

Scientists estimate the speed of dinosaurs by comparing their fossils to modern-day animals. Dinosaur footprints left in mud or sand can also tell us how fast dinosaurs could move.

Dinosaur fossils

Most fossils preserve the bones or other hard parts of an animal. Sometimes the footprints an animal made in sand or mud also became fossils.

Scientists learn about what dinosaurs ate by studying coprolites—fossilized dinosaur poop.

How does a fossil form?

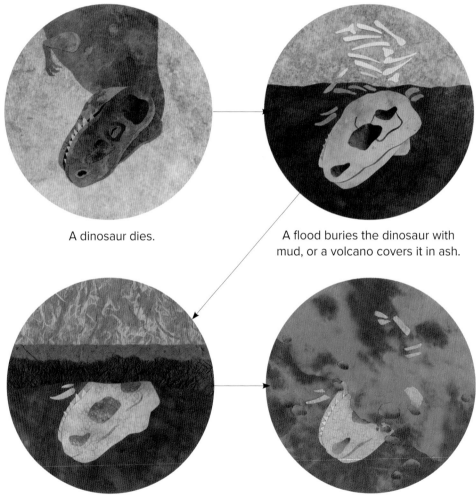

A dinosaur dies.

A flood buries the dinosaur with mud, or a volcano covers it in ash.

Minerals in the earth slowly turn the bones to stone.

Millions of years later, erosion uncovers the fossilized dinosaur bones.

Where have dinosaurs been found?

Each bone represents ten dinosaur fossil discoveries.

Asia

North America

South America

Europe

Africa

Australia

Antarctica

Building a dinosaur

It's rare to find the complete fossils of a dinosaur. Scientists recreated **Lythronax**—a relative of Tyrannosaurus rex—from just a few bones.

Lythronax fossil bones discovered

What color were the dinosaurs?

We don't really know. But scientists believe that some dinosaurs, like many modern birds and reptiles, were brightly colored.

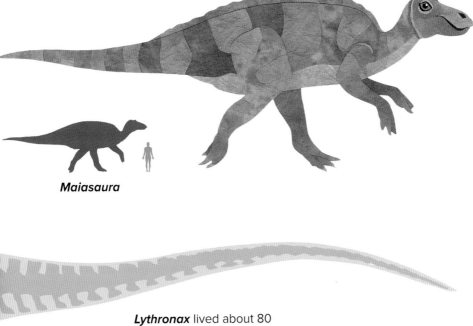

Maiasaura

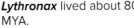

Lythronax lived about 80 MYA.

The leg bone of a **Patagotitan**, a giant plant-eating dinosaur. It is the largest fossil bone ever discovered.

Lythronax

Dinosaur claws

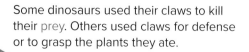

Some dinosaurs used their claws to kill their prey. Others used claws for defense or to grasp the plants they ate.

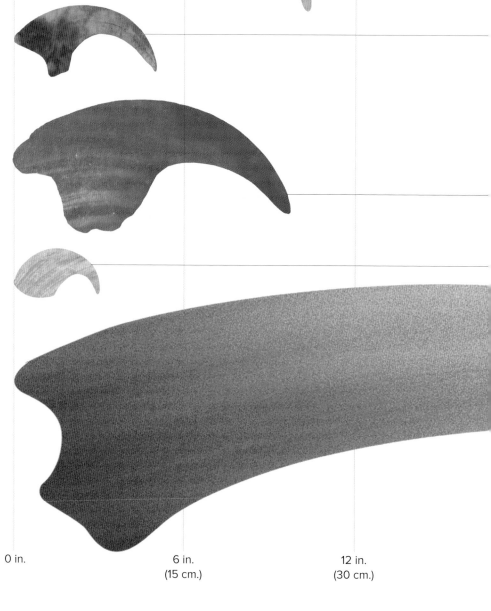

0 in.

6 in.
(15 cm.)

12 in.
(30 cm.)

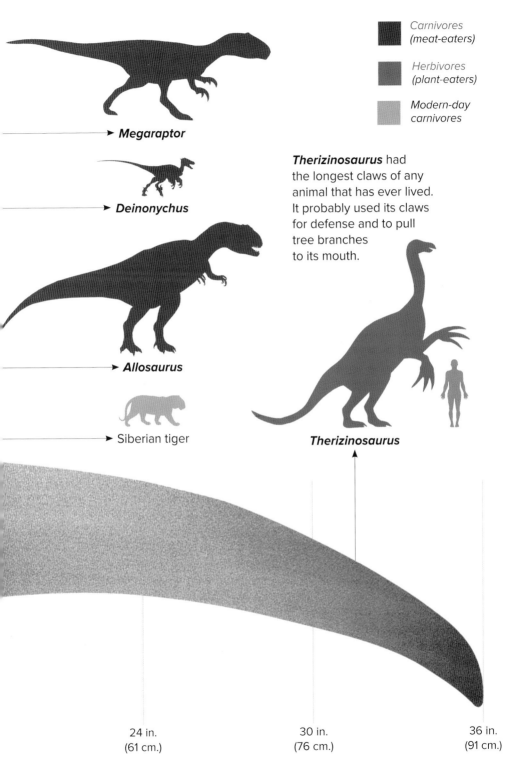

Carnivores
(meat-eaters)

Herbivores
(plant-eaters)

Modern-day
carnivores

Megaraptor

Deinonychus

Therizinosaurus had
the longest claws of any
animal that has ever lived.
It probably used its claws
for defense and to pull
tree branches
to its mouth.

Allosaurus

Siberian tiger

Therizinosaurus

24 in.
(61 cm.)

30 in.
(76 cm.)

36 in.
(91 cm.)

Dinosaur skulls

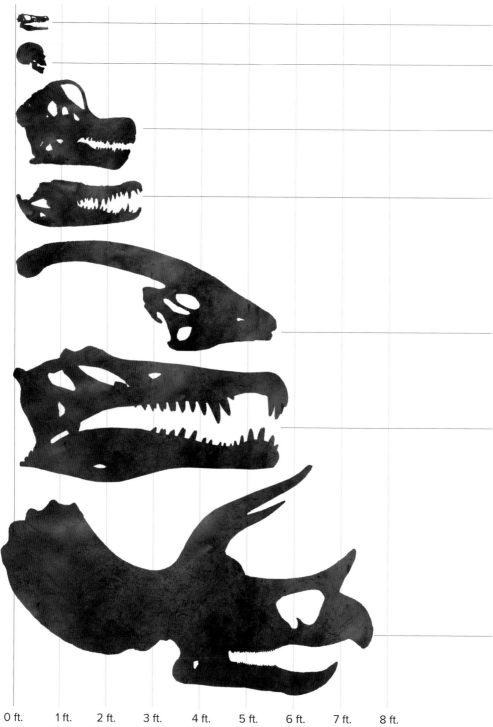

0 ft.   1 ft.   2 ft.   3 ft.   4 ft.   5 ft.   6 ft.   7 ft.   8 ft.
(30 cm.) (61 cm.) (91 cm.) (122 cm.) (152 cm.) (183 cm.) (213 cm.) (244 cm.)

Velociraptor

human

saltwater crocodile

Diplodocus

Parasaurolophus

Spinosaurus

Triceratops

Carnivores
(meat-eaters)

Herbivores
(plant-eaters)

Modern-day
animals

23

King of the dinosaurs

Tyrannosaurus rex is sometimes called
T. rex. It lived **66 MYA**, and it is probably
the best-known dinosaur.

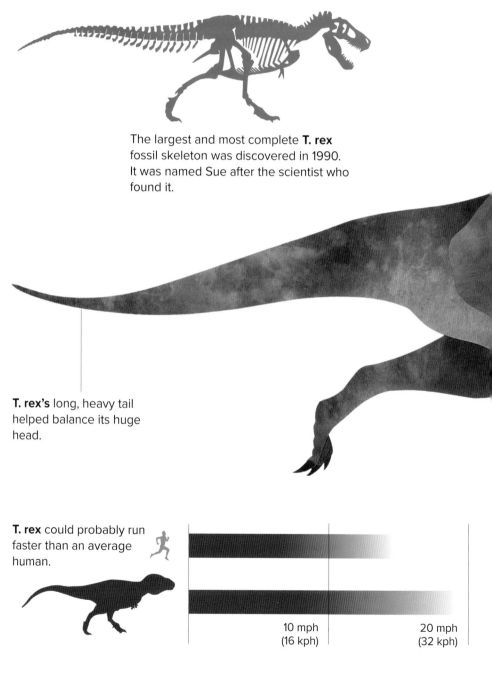

The largest and most complete **T. rex**
fossil skeleton was discovered in 1990.
It was named Sue after the scientist who
found it.

T. rex's long, heavy tail
helped balance its huge
head.

T. rex could probably run
faster than an average
human.

| 10 mph
(16 kph) | 20 mph
(32 kph) |

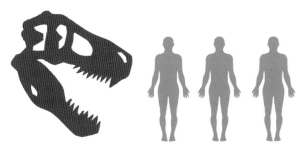

T. rex could swallow 500 pounds (227 kilograms) of meat in one gulp—as much as three adult humans.

T. rex fossils have been found in the western United States and Canada.

T. rex may have used its tiny arms to grasp its prey.

T. rex's huge mouth, sharp teeth, and powerful bite made it a top predator of its time.

Speedy thief

Velociraptor was a small but fierce predator. Its name means "speedy thief."

Velociraptor compared to an adult human

This dinosaur was covered with feathers, but it could not fly. Its feathers kept it warm. They might also have been used to signal a mate.

The first **Velociraptor** fossil was discovered in Mongolia in 1923.

Velociraptor was one of the fastest dinosaurs.

20 mph	40 mph
(32 kph)	(64 kph)

Velociraptors may have hunted in packs. By hunting together, they could have preyed on much larger dinosaurs.

Velociraptor lived about 75 MYA.

Velociraptor's killing claws were probably used to stab or slash its prey.

The killing claw shown life-size

The biggest of all?

Patagotitan is the largest dinosaur yet discovered. There may have been larger dinosaurs, but we have not found enough of their fossils to be sure.

Patagotitan moved about as fast as a person can walk.

5 mph
(8 kph)

Its long neck allowed **Patagotitan** to feed on leaves that other dinosaurs could not reach.

Patagotitan weighed as much as 14 African elephants—or 1,000 humans.

Patagotitan lived 95 MYA.

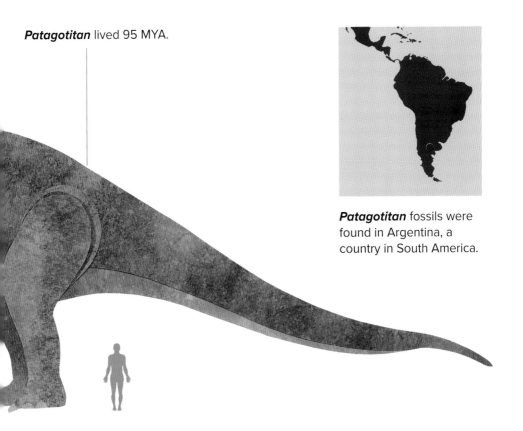

Patagotitan fossils were found in Argentina, a country in South America.

A tank on legs

Ankylosaurus was a slow-moving herbivore. But it was well-protected by its armored skin and a deadly weapon— its tail.

Ankylosaurus fossils were discovered in western North America.

With its bony tail club, **Ankylosaurus** could have shattered the bones of any predator, even a T. rex.

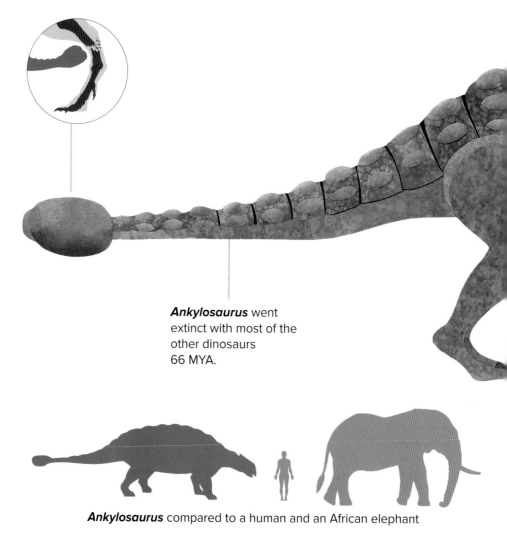

Ankylosaurus went extinct with most of the other dinosaurs 66 MYA.

Ankylosaurus compared to a human and an African elephant

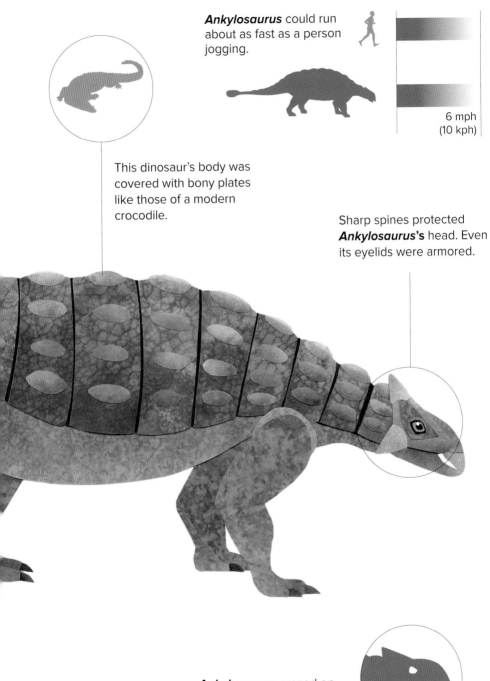

Ankylosaurus could run about as fast as a person jogging.

6 mph
(10 kph)

This dinosaur's body was covered with bony plates like those of a modern crocodile.

Sharp spines protected *Ankylosaurus*'s head. Even its eyelids were armored.

Ankylosaurus grazed on plants with its tough beak.

What killed the dinosaurs?

Sixty-six million years ago, an asteroid traveling at 20 times the speed of a bullet crashed into the earth.

UNITED STATES

GULF OF MEXICO

MEXICO

The asteroid landed in the ocean near what is now part of Mexico.

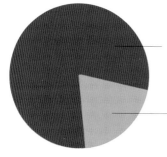

The asteroid's impact killed 8 out of every 10 animal species.

Animal species that survived the impact

The collision formed a crater 100 miles (160 kilometers) across.

The asteroid strike caused a series of deadly events.

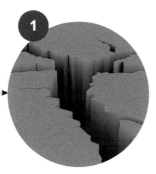

1 The shock caused powerful earthquakes.

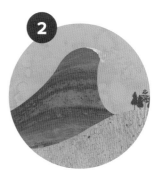

2 A tsunami as tall as a skyscraper swept across the land.

3 Red-hot debris from the impact started forest fires all over the globe.

4 The shock may have set off worldwide volcanic eruptions.

5 Dust, ash, and smoke blocked out the sunlight for years.

Massive lava flows in India at around the same time might have helped kill off the dinosaurs.

6 Without sunlight, plants could not survive. Soon the plant-eating dinosaurs died out. Without prey, the meat-eaters starved.

A vertebrate family tree

A vertebrate family tree (vertebrates are animals with backbones)

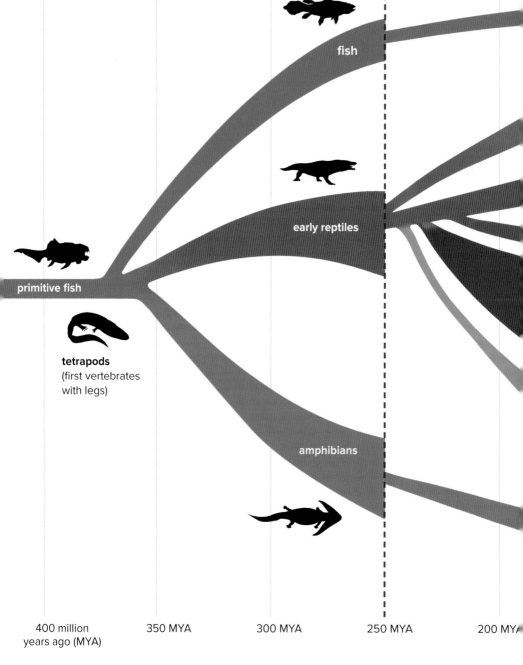

mass extinction
250 MYA

85% of all animals die

fish

early reptiles

primitive fish

tetrapods
(first vertebrates with legs)

amphibians

400 million years ago (MYA)

350 MYA

300 MYA

250 MYA

200 MYA

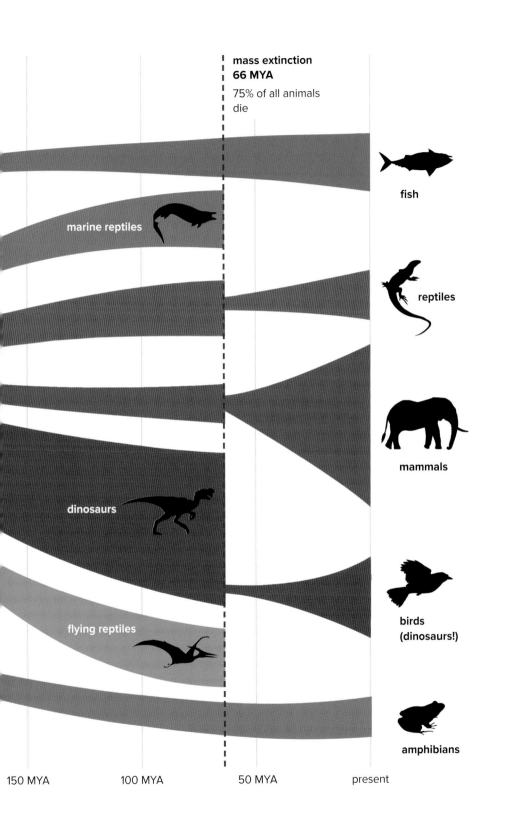

mass extinction
66 MYA
75% of all animals die

marine reptiles

fish

reptiles

dinosaurs

mammals

flying reptiles

birds
(dinosaurs!)

amphibians

150 MYA   100 MYA   50 MYA   present

Dinosaur facts

Here is more information about the dinosaurs in this book and a guide to pronouncing their names.

page 6
Lambeosaurus (lam-be-ah-**sor**-us)
A plant-eater that lived about 75 MYA (million years ago). 30 feet (9 meters) long.

pages 7, 14, 21
Allosaurus (al-oh-**sor**-us)
A predator that lived 150 MYA. 40 feet (12 meters) long.

page 8
Caudipteryx (caw-**dip**-ter-ix)
A small feathered dinosaur that lived 125 MYA. It probably ate plants and insects. 3 feet (90 centimeters) long.

page 9
Coelophysis (see-lo-**fie**-sis)
A speedy predator that ran on two legs and ate insects and small animals. It lived about 200 MYA. 10 feet (3 meters) long.

pages 9, 10, 13
Archeopteryx (ar-kay-**op**-teh-rix)
This feathered dinosaur was one of the first birds. It lived 150 MYA and probably ate insects and small reptiles. 20 inches (51 centimeters) long.

pages 10, 14, 23
Diplodocus (di-**plod**-oh-cus)
A huge herbivore (plant-eater) that lived 160 MYA. Its long neck allowed it to feed on vegetation that grew high above the ground. 85 feet (26 meters) long.

page 11
Utahraptor (you-tah-**rap**-tor)
This was the largest of the raptors. It was a fast, fierce predator, and it could prey on dinosaurs larger than it was. Utahraptor lived 125 MYA. 23 feet (7 meters) long.

pages 11, 12, 14, 23
Triceratops (tri-**seh**-rah-tops)
A large horned plant-eater. It died out at the time of the mass extinction 66 MYA. 30 feet (9 meters) long.

pages 12, 23
Parasaurolophus (pear-ah-sore-**ah**-loe-fus)
This herbivore could walk on both two legs and four legs. It lived 75 MYA. 30 feet (9 meters) long.

pages 12, 24, 25
Tyrannosaurus rex (ty-ran-ah-**sore**-us rex)
One of the largest predators of all time. Also known as T. rex, this dinosaur went extinct 66 MYA. 40 feet (12 meters) long.

pages 12, 30, 31
Ankylosaurus (an-ke-lo-**sore**-us)
A large armored dinosaur. It ate plants and defended itself with a bony club at the end of its tail. It died out 66 MYA. 20 feet (6 meters) long.

pages 12, 21
Therizinosaurus (ther-ih-zine-oh-**sore**-us)
An unusual-looking plant-eater. It had a big belly and extremely long claws on its front legs. It vanished in the mass extinction 66 MYA. 16 feet (5 meters) tall.

page 13
Stegosaurus (steg-oh-**sore**-us)
A plant-eater with a spiked tail and bony plates on its back. The spikes were used for defense, and the plates might have helped this dinosaur control its temperature. It lived 150 MYA. 30 feet (9 meters) long.

page 13
Dilophosaurus (di-**lahf**-o-**sore**-us)
A predator that lived 190 MYA. The crest on its head may have been used to signal other dinosaurs. 23 feet (7 meters) long.

page 13
Gallimimus (gal-ih-my-mus)
A feathered dinosaur that lived 70 MYA. It was a fast runner, and it was an omnivore—it ate both plants and animals. 13 feet (4 meters) long.

pages 13, 19
Maiasaura (my-ah-sore-ah)
One of the "duck-billed" dinosaurs. It was a large plant-eater that lived 75 MYA. It probably lived in large herds for protection against predators. 30 feet (9 meters) long.

pages 13, 23
Spinosaurus (spine-uh-sore-us)
Perhaps the largest predator to ever live on land. It could swim, and it ate fish and other animals. *Spinosaurus* lived 70 MYA. Estimates of its size vary, since we haven't found very many *Spinosaurus* fossils. 50 feet (15 meters) long.

pages 13, 14, 23, 26, 27
Velociraptor (vell-oss-eh-rap-tor)
A fast-running, feathered dinosaur. It was a predator, with a long, curved killing claw on each foot. It lived 75 MYA and may have hunted in packs. 6½ feet (2 meters) long.

pages 13, 19, 28, 29
Patagotitan (pat-ah-go-tie-tan)
This recently discovered dinosaur is, as far as we know, the largest land animal that ever lived. It lived 95 MYA and ate leaves, ferns, and other plants. 122 feet (37 meters) long.

pages 14, 15
Oviraptor (oh-vih-rap-tor)
A small, quick dinosaur. It was covered in feathers, and it may have been an omnivore, eating plants, insects, and small animals. It lived 75 MYA, and built nests for its eggs, much like modern birds. 6 feet (180 centimeters) long.

pages 18, 19
Lythronax (ly-thruh-nax)
A large predator that lived 80 MYA. Like its relative *Tyrannosaurus rex*, it had small arms and large, powerful jaws. 24 feet (7½ meters) long.

page 21
Deinonychus (die-non-ih-cus)
A predator that ran on two legs and used its teeth and long claws to kill its prey. It lived 125 MYA. 8 feet (2½ meters) long.

page 21
Megaraptor (meg-ah-rap-tor)
A large, fast-running predatory dinosaur that lived 85 MYA. It had long, deadly claws on its hands. 36 feet (11 meters) long.

A note about dinosaur dates and sizes

We know when dinosaurs lived by studying their fossils. But only a small fraction of animals leave fossils behind, and estimates of when a particular kind of dinosaur lived may miss the ones that lived earlier or later. Many of the dinosaurs in this book were around for millions of years, so the single dates given above are just a rough guide to when these creatures existed.

Determining size is also tricky. We don't know if we've found fossils of the largest dinosaur of a particular kind—maybe a larger one will be discovered. Or perhaps we are looking at the fossils of a dinosaur that was not fully grown. But as we find and study more fossils, our estimates of dates and sizes will become more accurate.

Glossary

armored
Covered with protective plates or scales.

asteroid
A rocky, irregularly shaped object that circles the sun. Asteroids range from a few hundred feet to 600 miles (965 kilometers) across.

carnivore
An animal that eats the flesh of other animals.

debris
Pieces or fragments of something that has exploded, been broken, or fallen apart.

erosion
The gradual wearing away of the earth's surface by the action of wind, rain, and ice.

evolved
In animals, a gradual change in form and behavior from one generation to the next. With enough time, entirely new kinds of animals appear.

extinct
No longer living.

fossils
The preserved remains or traces of ancient plants and animals.

herbivore
An animal—or human—that eats plants but does not eat other animals.

human ancestors
Relatives of modern humans that lived between two million and 200,000 years ago.

infographics
Facts and information presented visually as diagrams, charts, and graphs rather than just text.

kilograms
A unit of weight in the metric system. One kilogram is 2.2 pounds.

kilometers per hour
The kilometer is a metric unit of distance equal to $6/10$ of a mile. Kilometers per hour (kph) measures the distance (in kilometers) traveled in one hour.

lava flows
Rivers or sheets of red-hot, melted rock that flow from a volcano or from a volcanic vent.

mass extinction
An event that kills at least half of all living plant and animal species. There have been at least five mass extinctions over the past 450 million years.

minerals
Solid, non-living substances formed in the earth. Rocks, salt, and metals, such as silver and gold, are examples of minerals.

Mongolia
A country in Asia. It lies between China to the south and Russia to the north.

omnivore
An animal that eats both plants and other animals.

predators
Animals that kill and eat other animals.

prey
An animal that is hunted and eaten by other animals.

reptile
A group of egg-laying animals with scaly skin, including turtles, lizards, snakes, and crocodiles.

scientific names
A system of naming living things that is based on the Latin language.

species
A group of living things that look alike, behave in a similar way, and are able to produce offspring.

tsunami
Large, dangerous ocean waves caused by earthquakes, underwater landslides, volcanoes, or impacts from meteors or asteroids.

warm-blooded
Animals that can keep their body at a constant temperature, often warmer than the environment.

Bibliography

Digging for Bird Dinosaurs: An Expedition to Madagascar. By Nic Bishop. Houghton Mifflin, 2000.

Dinosaurs. Edited by Sherry Gerstein and Beverly Larsen. Reader's Digest Children's Books, 1999.

Dinosaurs: A Concise Natural History. By David E. Fastovsky and David B. Weishampel. Cambridge University Press, 2016.

Dinosaur Encyclopedia. Edited by Kitty Blount and Maggie Crowley. DK Publishing, 2001.

Dinosaurs: How They Lived and Evolved. By Darren Nash and Paul Barrett. Smithsonian Book, 2016.

Encyclopedia of Dinosaurs and Other Prehistoric Creatures. Edited by James Pickering. Backpack Books, 2002.

Little Kids First Big Book of Dinosaurs. By Catherine D. Hughes. National Geographic Children's Books, 2011.

Prehistoric Predators. By Brian Switek. Applesauce Press, 2015.

The Ultimate Book of Dinosaurs. By Paul Dowswell, John Malam, Paul Mason, and Steve Parker. Paragon Publishing, 2003.

For Allen Ray

clarionbooks.com

The illustrations are cut- and torn-paper collage.
The infographics are cut-paper silhouettes and graphics created digitally.
The text type was set in Proxima Nova.
The display type was set in Berthold Akzidenz Grotesk.

ISBN: 978-1-328-85095-9 hardcover
ISBN: 978-1-328-85096-6 paperback

Manufactured in China
22 SCP 10 9 8 7 6